For Murphy
and Toby

On the first day of Christmas
my mama gave to me
A new stinky brother

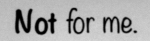
Not for me.

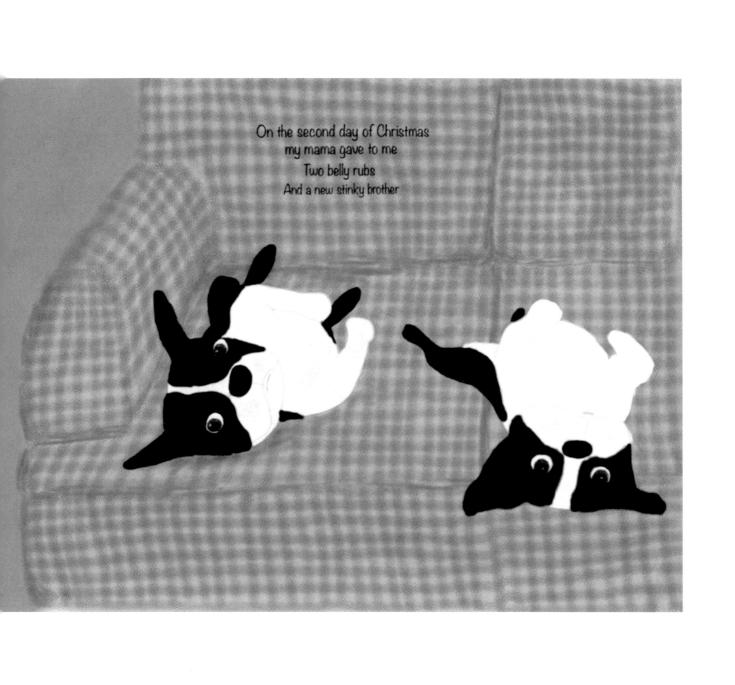

On the second day of Christmas
my mama gave to me
Two belly rubs
And a new stinky brother

On the third day of Christmas
my mama gave to me
Three strings of lights
Two belly rubs
And a new stinky brother

On the fourth day of Christmas
my mama gave to me
Four squirrels teasing
Three strings of lights
Two belly rubs
And a new stinky brother

On the fifth day of Christmas
my mama gave to me
Five frisbees flying
Four squirrels teasing
Three strings of lights
Two belly rubs
And a new stinky brother

On the sixth day of Christmas
my mama gave to me
Six songs a singing
Five frisbees flying
Four squirrels teasing
Three strings of lights
Two belly rubs
And a new stinky brother

On the seventh day of Christmas
my mama gave to me
Seven bedtime stories
Six songs a singing
Five frisbees flying
Four squirrels teasing
Three strings of lights
Two belly rubs
And a new stinky brother

On the eighth day of Christmas
my mama gave to me
Eight boots for wearing
Seven bedtime stories
Six songs a singing
Five frisbees flying
Four squirrels teasing
Three strings of lights
Two belly rubs
And a new stinky brother

Let
it
Snow

On the ninth day of Christmas
my mama gave to me
Nine Christmas cookies
Eight boots for wearing
Seven bedtime stories
Six songs a singing
Five frisbees flying
Four squirrels teasing
Three strings of lights
Two belly rubs
And a new stinky brother

On the tenth day of Christmas
my mama gave to me
Ten snowflakes falling
Nine Christmas cookies
Eight boots for wearing
Seven bedtime stories
Six songs a singing
Five frisbees flying
Four squirrels teasing
Three strings of lights
Two belly rubs
And a new stinky brother

On the eleventh day of Christmas
my mama gave to me
Eleven balls a bouncing
Ten snowflakes falling
Nine Christmas cookies
Eight boots for wearing
Seven bedtime stories
Six songs a singing
Five frisbees flying
Four squirrels teasing
Three strings of lights
Two belly rubs
And a new stinky brother

On the twelfth day of Christmas
my mama gave to me
Twelve stars a twinkling
Eleven balls a bouncing
Ten snowflakes falling
Nine Christmas cookies
Eight boots for wearing
Seven bedtime stories
Six songs a singing
Five frisbees flying
Four squirrels teasing
Three strings of lights
Two belly rubs

Murphy's Mission

Murphy's goal in life was to love and spread joy. By creating Murphy's Mission it is our hopes to continue his message. By purchasing this book you will be helping the many animals that are still waiting for families like yours.

For each book sold, Murphy's Mission will donate one dollar to a non-profit rescue organization. To learn more about Murphy's Mission and what organizations we are contributing to, please visit the About section on our Facebook page.

www.Facebook.com/MurphysBooks

Made in the USA
Monee, IL
24 November 2020